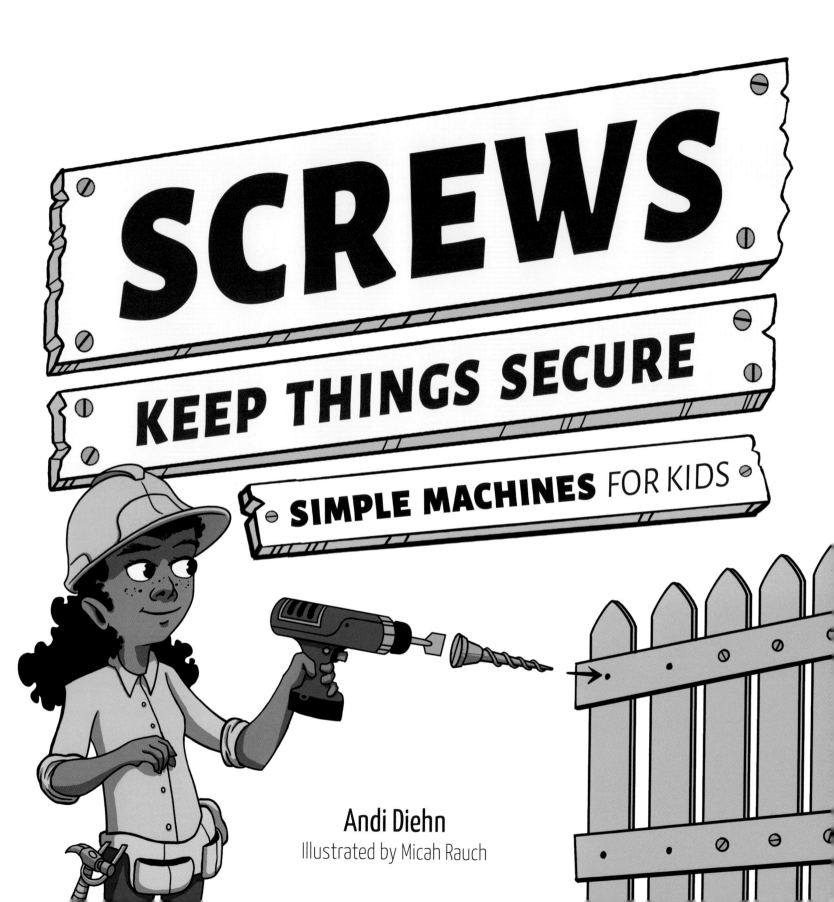

SCREWS

KEEP THINGS SECURE

SIMPLE MACHINES FOR KIDS

Andi Diehn

Illustrated by Micah Rauch

EXPLORE THE BIOMES IN THIS PICTURE BOOK SCIENCE SET!

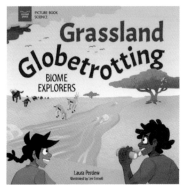

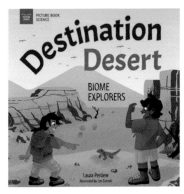

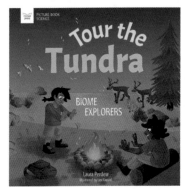

Check out more titles at www.nomadpress.net

Nomad Press

A division of Nomad Communications

10 9 8 7 6 5 4 3 2

This book was manufactured by CGB Printers,
North Mankato, Minnesota, United States

ISBN Softcover: 978-1-64741-094-0
ISBN Hardcover: 978-1-64741-091-9

Educational Consultant, Marla Conn

Questions regarding the ordering of this book should be addressed to
Nomad Press
PO Box 1036, Norwich, VT 05055
www.nomadpress.net

Printed in the United States.

When we built a treehouse,

We used screws to hold it together.

Screws in the walls, screws in the roof, screws in the floor.

Twist and turn, tighten and twist.

Now, we sit on beanbag chairs in our treehouse.

The breeze outside knocks and asks, "Let me in?"

And our door, 20 screws strong, waits for us to decide.

Sure! Come on in, breeze, and visit our treehouse!

If you were building a treehouse,
what could you use to keep
the boards together?

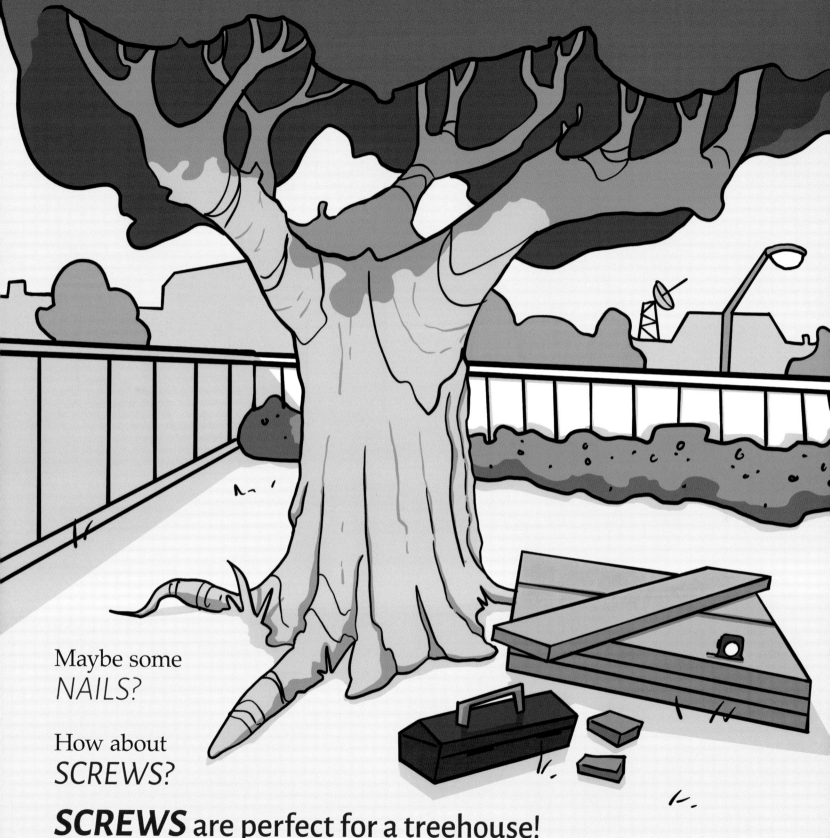

Maybe some *NAILS?*

How about *SCREWS?*

SCREWS are perfect for a treehouse!

The kinds of **screws** you use in your treehouse are **fasteners.**
They **connect** solid materials and **hold them together**.

They're a
good tool for
building the wooden
WALLS,
FLOOR, and
ROOF of a treehouse!

Have you ever looked closely at a screw?
What do you notice about it?

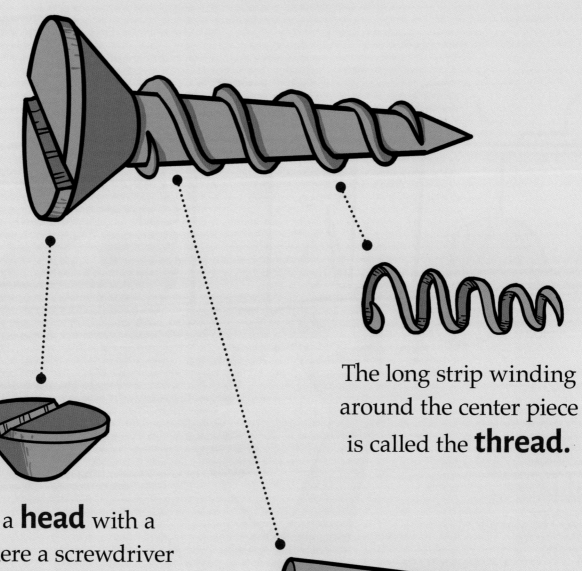

The long strip winding
around the center piece
is called the **thread.**

There's a **head** with a
notch where a screwdriver
can fit and help you
turn the screw.

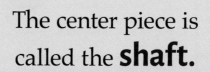

The center piece is
called the **shaft.**

As you turn the screwdriver,
the **thread** on the screw
cuts a path through the wood,
making the screw
STICK TIGHT!

The **closer together the threads** are on the screw, the **better it will hold** two materials together.

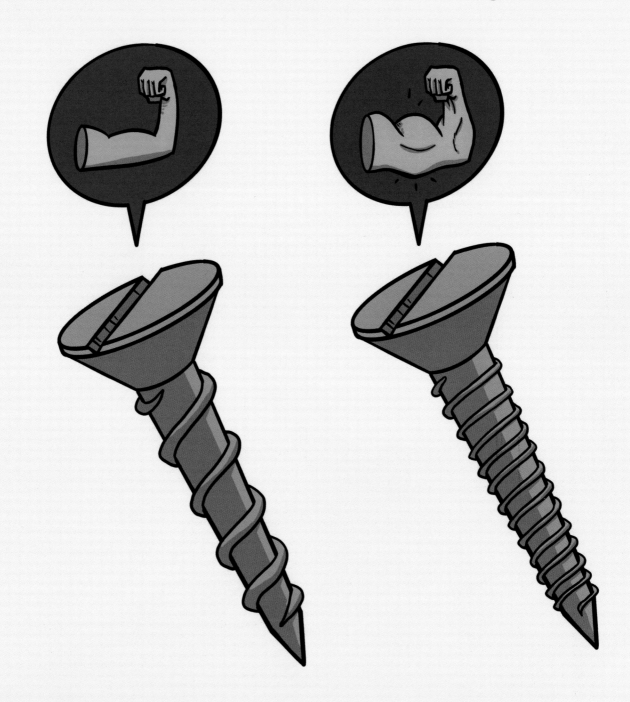

But it will take **more work,** or **more turns** of the screwdriver, to get the screw in place.

A screw is a **simple machine.**

A simple machine is a device that helps us do work. It does this by giving us a **mechanical advantage.**

A mechanical advantage makes your pushing and pulling force much more powerful than when you use only your own muscles.

How does mechanical advantage work with a screw?

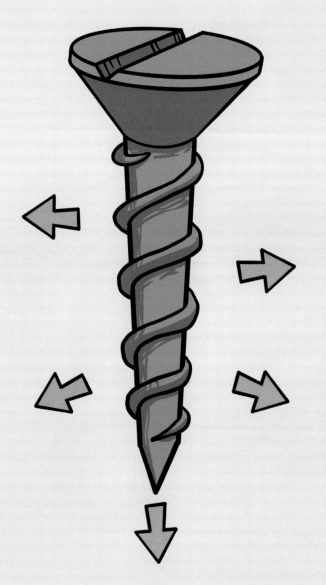

A screw spreads out a force along the

WHOLE LENGTH

of the thread, making it
more secure in the wood.

A screw uses **another** simple machine.
The thread that winds around the shaft
is an **inclined plane,**
also called a ramp.

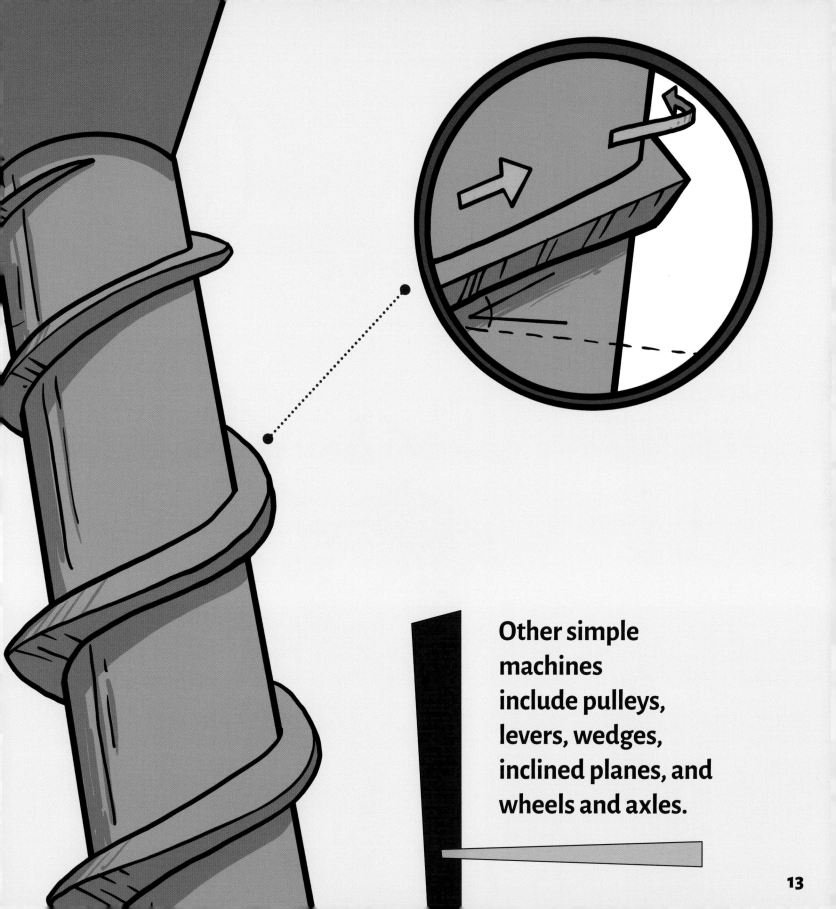

Other simple
machines
include pulleys,
levers, wedges,
inclined planes, and
wheels and axles.

What do you see when you twist off the cap of your water bottle?

A screw top!

Look inside the cap and find the **threads**. These threads fit into matching GROOVES on the outside of the bottle top.

When you screw the cap back on, it forms a TIGHT SEAL, so water doesn't leak inside your backpack!

Many liquids are kept in
bottles with screw tops.
**Look around your kitchen
and see what you can find.**

Don't forget to screw
all the tops back on!

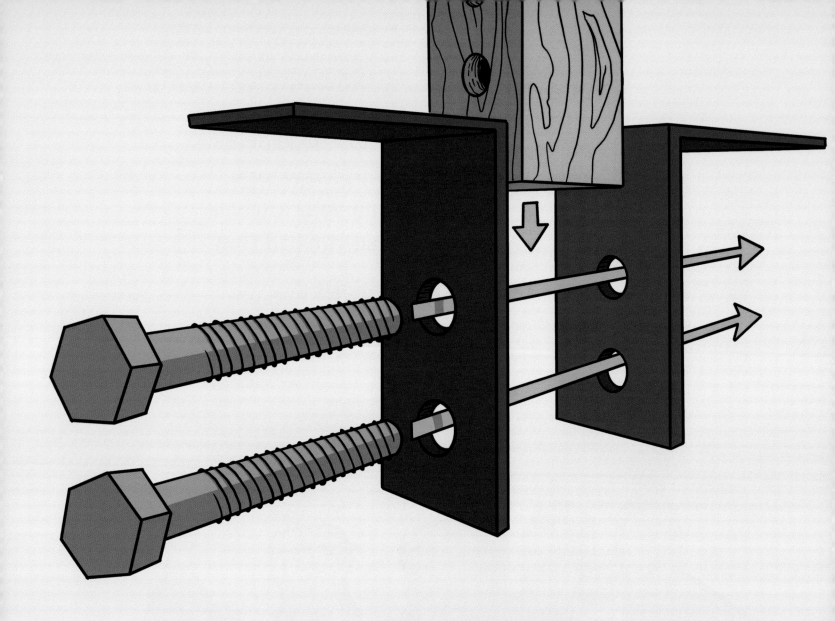

Have you ever seen a bolt used
to hold something together?

A **bolt** is another kind of
fastener with a thread
circling a **central shaft**.

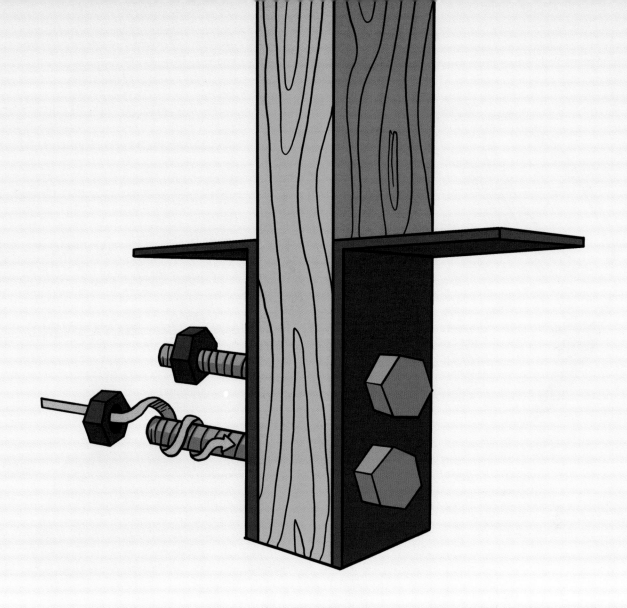

But you don't screw bolts into other materials.

Instead, you use them with a **nut.**
The nut screws onto the bolt. Whatever
is being held in place is SQUISHED
between the nut and bolt.

Look at the back of a watch or calculator.

What do you see holding those tiny pieces together?

Screws!

Have you ever replaced
a burnt-out lightbulb?

How does the lightbulb
stay in place?

Lightbulbs have a
built-in screw!

Many of the screws we see every day are small, and some are very tiny.

People use

enormous
screws

for different kinds of jobs.

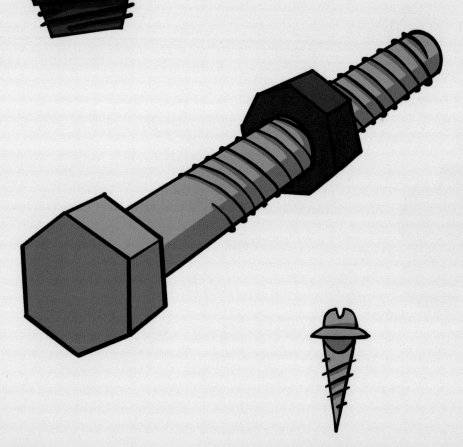

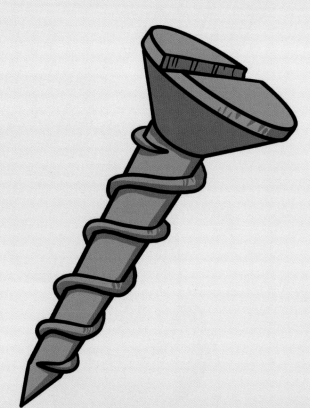

These screws **move large amounts of material**—such as dirt or concrete—along their threads from one end of the shaft to the other.

These are called **screw conveyors.**

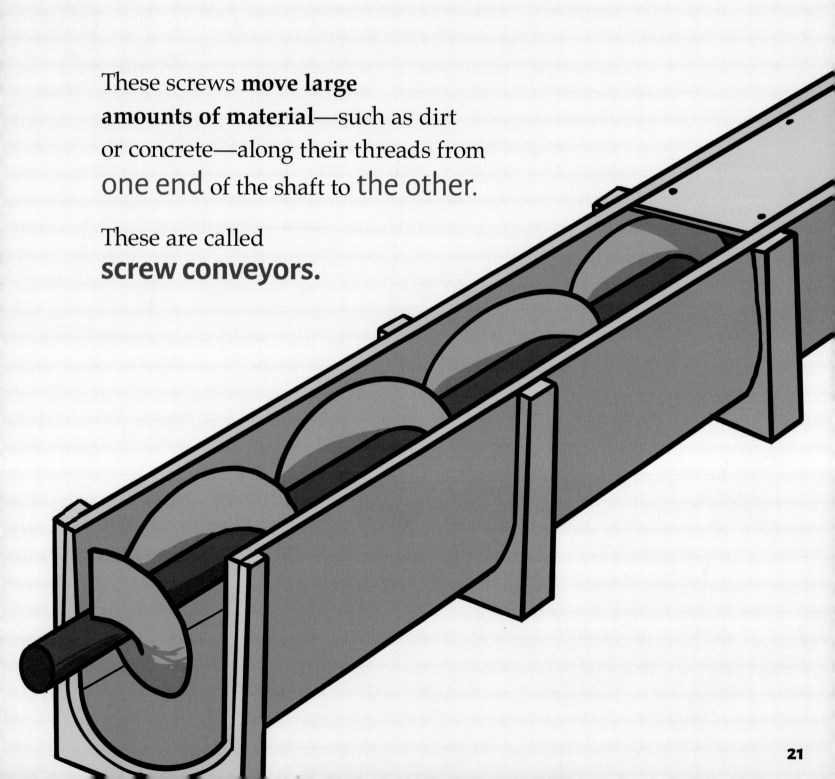

An early kind of screw conveyor
is called an **Archimedes' screw.**

Archimedes was the ancient Greek thinker
who first described this type of screw.

Here's how an Archimedes' screw works.

One end of the screw is placed in the water and the screw is turned. As the screw threads move around and around, they carry the water UP THE SLOPE.

BRILLIANT!

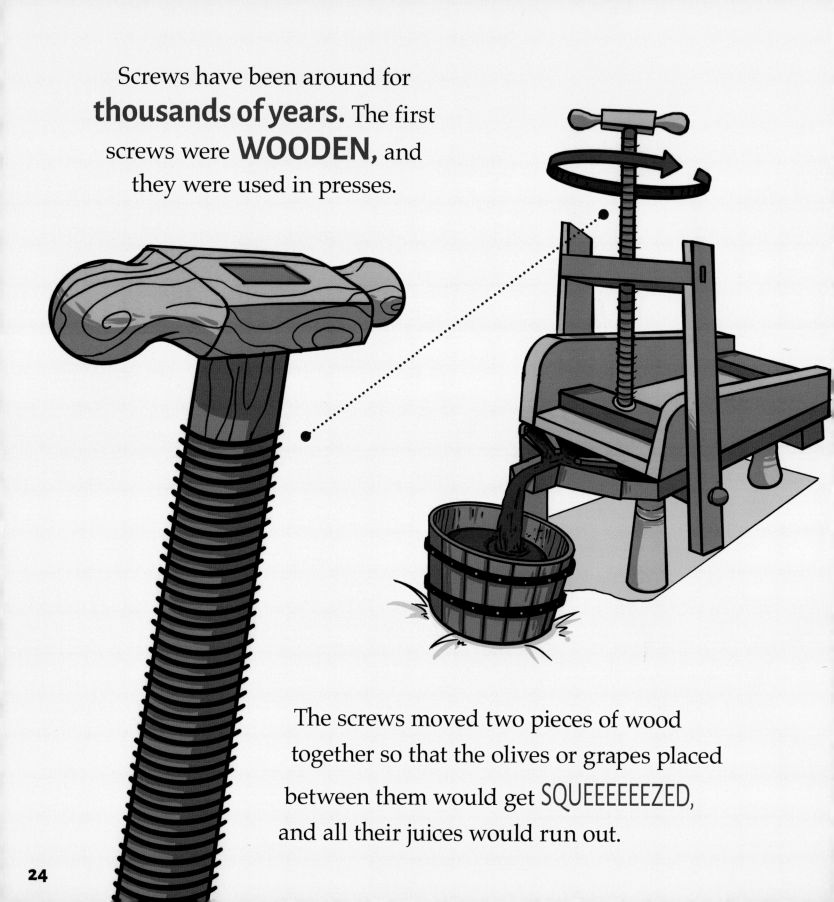

Screws have been around for **thousands of years.** The first screws were **WOODEN,** and they were used in presses.

The screws moved two pieces of wood together so that the olives or grapes placed between them would get SQUEEEEEEZED, and all their juices would run out.

These wooden screws were made by hand and took a VERY LONG TIME to make. They were **never** the same *shape* and size.

About 300 years ago, people invented a machine called a **lathe** that could make screws VERY QUICKLY—

All the same *shape and size.*

That's when people began to use screws as fasteners.

Later, people began to make **metal screws.**

Now, we have special screws for
WOOD,

METAL,

CONCRETE,

PLASTIC—all
different kinds of
building materials!

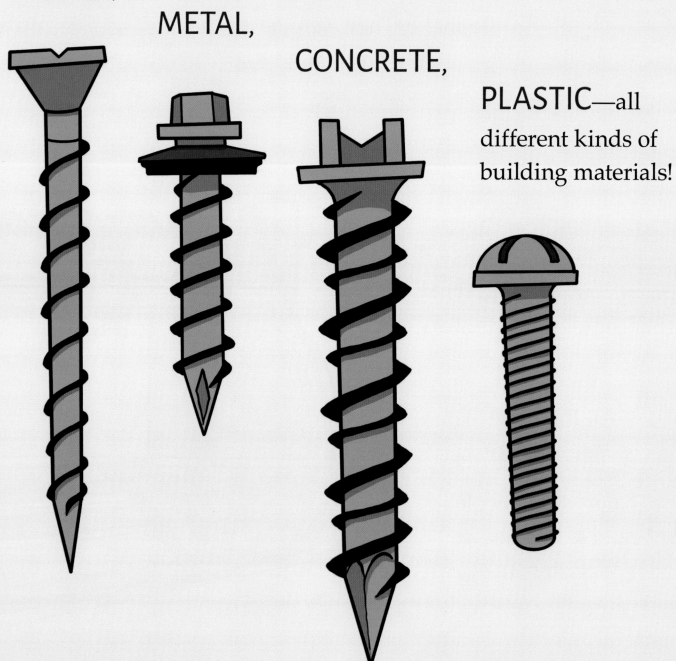

Look around your house—where can you
see screws doing very important jobs?

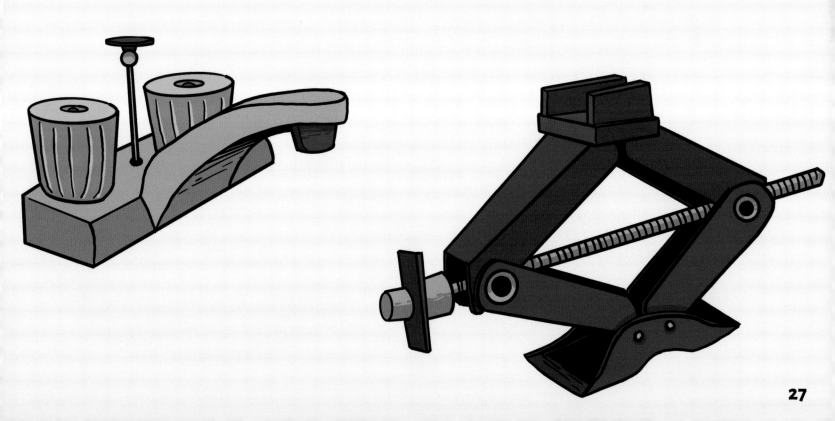

Make an Archimedes' Screw!

What You Need

clear flexible tubing - a piece of plastic pipe or a long can - clear tape - bowl of water - food coloring

What You Do

- Wrap the clear tubing around your pipe or can. Keep it in place with the clear tape. This is your Archimedes' screw.

- Splash a few drops of food coloring into the bowl of water.

- Set one end of your Archimedes' screw into the bowl of water and, keeping the screw at an angle, start turning it so that water gets scooped up into the tubing.

What Happens?

How does the water travel up the tubing?

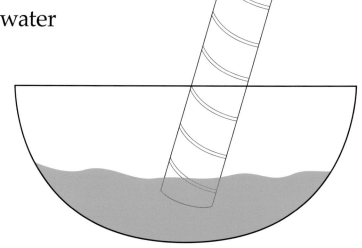

Glossary

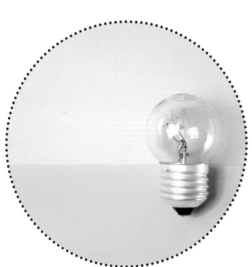

bolt: a strong screw used with a nut to fasten things.

force: a push or pull that changes an object's motion.

inclined plane: a sloped surface that connects a lower level to a higher level.

lathe: a machine that removes material from an object as it spins.

lever: a bar that rests on a support and lifts or moves things.

load: an applied force or weight.

mechanical advantage: the amount a machine increases or changes a force to make a task easier.

nut: a donut-shape with screw threads on the inner circle used with a bolt through the center to hold things together.

pulley: a wheel with a grooved rim that a rope or chain is pulled through to help lift a load.

screw: a simple machine that has an inclined plane wrapped around a central axis. It is used to lift objects or hold things together.

shaft: the long, narrow part of an object.

simple machine: a device that changes the direction or strength of a force. The six simple machines are the inclined plane, lever, pulley, screw, wedge, and wheel and axle.

slope: a surface that has one end or side at a higher level than the other.

thread: the raised edge of a screw that winds around.

wedge: thick at one end and narrow at the other, a wedge is used for splitting, tightening, and securing objects.

wheel and axle: a wheel with a rod that turn together to lift and move loads.

work: the force applied to an object to move it across a distance.

Inclined Plane

Wedge

Lever

SIMPLE MACHINES

Pulley

Screw

Wheel and Axle